The Life Cycle Series

The Life Cycle of a
Beetle

Molly Aloian & Bobbie Kalman

Crabtree Publishing Company

www.crabtreebooks.com

The Life Cycle Series

A Bobbie Kalman Book

Dedicated by Molly Aloian
For Susan, a beautiful person and a wonderful friend

Editor-in-Chief
Bobbie Kalman

Writing team
Molly Aloian
Bobbie Kalman

Substantive editor
Kathryn Smithyman

Editors
Amanda Bishop
Kelley MacAulay
Rebecca Sjonger

Art director
Robert MacGregor

Design
Margaret Amy Reiach

Production coordinator
Heather Fitzpatrick

Photo research
Crystal Foxton

Consultant
Patricia Loesche, Ph.D., Animal Behavior Program,
Department of Psychology, University of Washington

Photographs
© Dwight R. Kuhn: page 26 (right)
Robert McCaw: pages 3, 6, 13 (left), 14, 16, 18, 20, 22 (right), 23,
    29 (bottom), 30, 31
Allen Blake Sheldon: pages 1, 8 (top), 26 (left), 27, 29 (top)
Tom Stack & Associates: Joe McDonald: page 10 (top)
Visuals Unlimited: Ken Lucas: pages 8 (bottom), 28; Sylvan H. Wittwer:
    page 11 (top); Bill Beatty: pages 11 (bottom), 12, 15, 22 (left), 24,
    25 (top); Tom Edwards: page 13 (right); Jerome Wexler: page 17;
    Science VU: pages 19, 25 (bottom); Jeff J. Daly: page 21 (top)
Other images by Digital Stock and Digital Vision

Illustrations
Barbara Bedell: front cover, series logo, border (ladybird beetle),
    pages 5 (darkling beetle), 6, 7 (ant), 9, 16, 27 (bottom)
Margaret Amy Reiach: page 7 (butterfly & grasshopper)
Bonna Rouse: back cover, border (except ladybird beetle), pages 4,
    5 (except darkling beetle), 7 (top), 27 (top), 31
Tiffany Wybouw: page 7 (wasp)

Digital Prepress
Embassy Graphics

Printer
Worzalla Publishing Company

Crabtree Publishing Company

www.crabtreebooks.com   1-800-387-7650

PMB 16A   612 Welland Avenue   73 Lime Walk
350 Fifth Avenue   St. Catharines   Headington
Suite 3308   Ontario   Oxford
New York, NY   Canada   OX3 7AD
10118   L2M 5V6   United Kingdom

Cataloging-in-Publication Data
Aloian, Molly.
    The life cycle of a beetle / Molly Aloian & Bobbie Kalman.
    p. cm. -- (The life cycle series)
    ISBN 0-7787-0662-1 (RLB) -- ISBN 0-7787-0692-3 (pbk.)
    1. Beetles--Life cycles--Juvenile literature. [1. Beetles.]
I. Kalman, Bobbie. II. Title.
    QL576.2.A58 2003
    595.76--dc22
                                                    2003024985
                                                    LC

Contents

Bunches of beetles

Beetles have lived on Earth for more than 250 million years. They are found in every part of the world except Antarctica. Beetles live in deserts, in rain forests, on mountains, and underground. Some beetles even live in water! There are at least 350,000 different **species**, or types, of beetles living on Earth. Each year, scientists discover thousands of new species. Beetles come in many colors, sizes, and shapes. Some are more than six inches (15 cm) long, whereas others are less than one-quarter of an inch (3 mm) long.

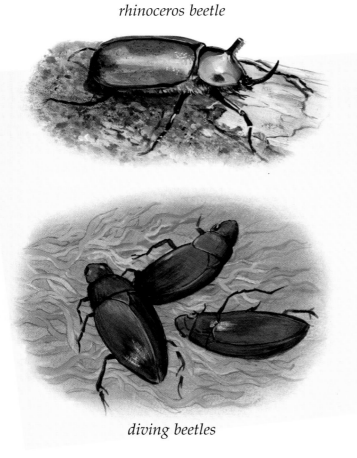

rhinoceros beetle

diving beetles

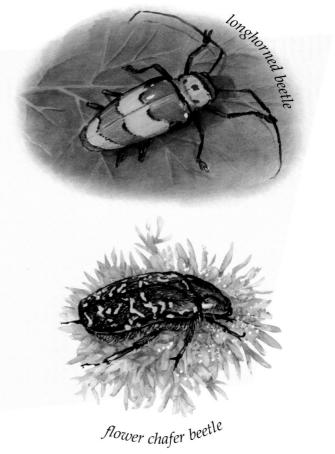

longhorned beetle

flower chafer beetle

jewel beetle

snout beetles

darkling beetle

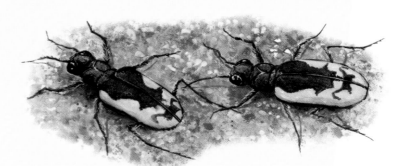
tiger beetles

scarab beetles

scarab beetle
flying

What is a beetle?

A beetle is an **insect**. Insects are small animals with six legs and three body parts. Like all insects, beetles are **arthropods**. The word "arthropod" means "hinged feet." All arthropods have joints that bend. Arthropods are **invertebrates**, which means they do not have backbones. Instead, every arthropod has a hard outer covering called an **exoskeleton**.

About insects

Some insects have wings. Most beetles have wings. Beetles also have two feelers called **antennae**, or antennas. Beetles feel, smell, taste, and sense movement with their antennae. The antennae of some beetles are almost three times as long as their bodies!

The dogbane beetle's shiny exoskeleton may appear blue, green, or copper in color.

A beetle's body

A beetle's eyes, antennae, and **mandibles**, or mouthparts, are on its head. The wings and legs are on the beetle's **thorax**. A beetle uses its legs for walking, running, and digging. Some beetles also use their legs for swimming, jumping, or landing from flight. A beetle's **organs** are inside its **abdomen**. The organs are protected by the tough exoskeleton.

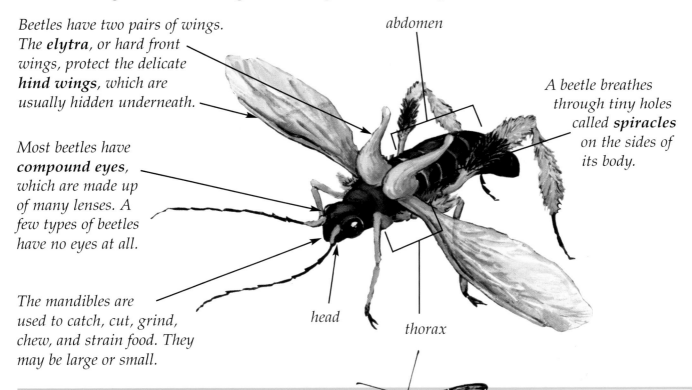

*Beetles have two pairs of wings. The **elytra**, or hard front wings, protect the delicate **hind wings**, which are usually hidden underneath.*

*Most beetles have **compound eyes**, which are made up of many lenses. A few types of beetles have no eyes at all.*

The mandibles are used to catch, cut, grind, chew, and strain food. They may be large or small.

abdomen

*A beetle breathes through tiny holes called **spiracles** on the sides of its body.*

head

thorax

wasp

fly

butterfly

grasshopper

ant

Beetle relatives

Beetles are related to other insects such as ants, butterflies, grasshoppers, flies, and wasps. All insects have the same basic body parts—a head, an abdomen, and a thorax. The thoraxes of beetles are made up of two parts, whereas those of other insects are made up of only one part.

What is a life cycle?

There are about 2,800 different species of net-winged beetles.

All animals go through a **life cycle**. A life cycle is made up of the **stages**, or changes, in an animal's life. First, the animal is born or hatches from an egg. It then changes and grows until it becomes an adult. As adults, animals can **reproduce**, or make babies. When an adult has babies, a new life cycle begins. All beetles go through these stages and changes during their life cycles. Depending on their **life spans,** some beetles move through the stages more quickly than others do.

Life span

An animal's life span is the length of time that animal is alive. Different beetles have different life spans. Some live for just one month. A few, including certain longhorned beetles, can live as long as 30 years. These beetles go through their life cycles much more slowly than other beetles do.

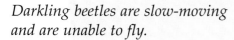

Darkling beetles are slow-moving and are unable to fly.

A beetle's life cycle

Every beetle begins its life inside an egg. A baby beetle that hatches from an egg is called a **larva**. As soon as the larva hatches, it begins to eat. As it eats and grows bigger, it **molts**, or sheds, its skin and grows a new one. Once the larva is fully grown, it makes a hard protective case around itself. It is now a **pupa**.

The pupa does not look like an adult beetle. Its body goes through a series of changes while it is a pupa. This series of changes is called **metamorphosis**. As soon as the pupa's body is finished changing, its case splits open and an adult beetle crawls out. A fully grown female beetle can lay eggs. With each egg, a new life cycle begins.

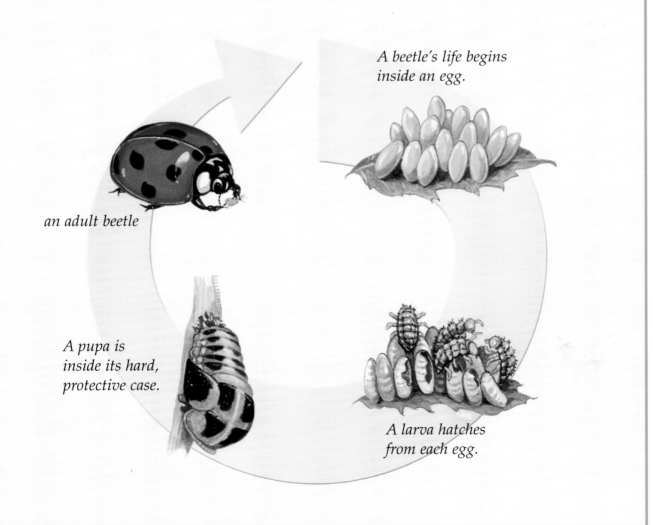

an adult beetle

A beetle's life begins inside an egg.

A pupa is inside its hard, protective case.

A larva hatches from each egg.

Almost all adult female beetles are **oviparous**, which means they lay eggs. Many beetles begin laying eggs in spring or summer. Some lay thousands of eggs at a time, whereas others lay only a few eggs at a time.

Dung beetles roll animal droppings into tight balls. Female dung beetles lay their eggs in the balls. The **larvae**, *or larvas, start feeding on the droppings as soon as they hatch.*

All about eggs

All beetle eggs are tiny. Most are white or pale yellow, soft, smooth, and oval. Many beetles lay **clusters**, or groups, of eggs.

Places to lay eggs

Before laying her eggs, a female must find a safe, protected spot. The eggs need to be hidden from **predators**, or animals that feed on them. The eggs also need to be laid near a food source so the larvae will have enough to eat when they hatch from the eggs.

Some eggs, including ladybird beetle eggs, are covered with a sticky coating. The coating protects the eggs and helps them stay attached to surfaces such as leaves or stems.

Living on yolk

Each egg contains an **embryo**, or developing baby, and a large amount of **yolk**. The yolk provides **nutrients**, or food energy, for the embryo while its body develops. The embryo hatches when it outgrows the egg.

Keeping eggs inside

Some female beetles do not lay their eggs. Instead, the female carries the eggs inside her body. When the eggs are ready, they hatch and the larvae **emerge** from, or come out of, the female's body.

Some beetles lay their eggs inside plant stems or in the folds of leaves.

Safe and sound

Most beetles do not guard their eggs. They protect them in other ways. Dung beetles and carrion beetles lay eggs in burrows to hide them and keep them safe from predators. Water scavenger beetles often lay their eggs in silk cases that they attach to water plants. The Colorado potato beetle, shown right, sticks its eggs to the undersides of leaves so predators cannot see them.

Bursting out

After about one week inside their eggs, most larvae are ready to hatch. All the eggs in a cluster hatch at about the same time.

Breaking through

The larvae break through their eggs using their powerful mandibles. Some larvae have special **spines**, or spikes, on their heads or abdomens, which also help break through the eggs. These spines are called "egg bursters."

Different larvae

The larvae of different beetles are various shapes, lengths, and colors. Some have plump, curved bodies, whereas others have bodies that are long and slender. Larvae may be pale white or dark brown in color. They can be hairless or hairy. Beetle larvae usually do not have wings or elytra, but most species have antennae, mouthparts, and legs. Some are fast runners, whereas others move slowly.

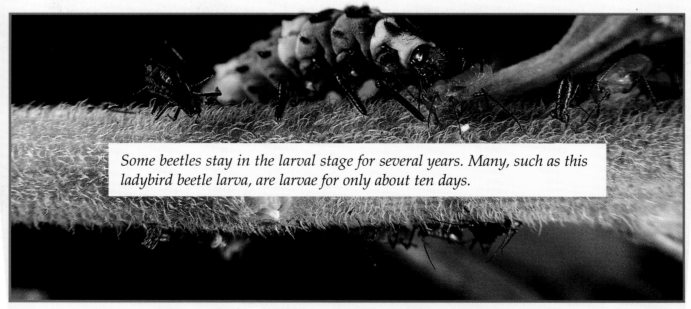

Some beetles stay in the larval stage for several years. Many, such as this ladybird beetle larva, are larvae for only about ten days.

Food for larvae

The larvae start eating as soon as they hatch. In fact, they spend most of their time eating! What the larvae eat depends on where they live. Scarab beetle larvae live in soil, so they feed on roots, sap, and rotting wood. Longicorn beetle larvae live in wood and eat the wood as they tunnel through it. Other larvae eat **aphids**, sticks, leaves, dead insects or animals, and even animal droppings.

*Woodboring beetle larvae use their strong mandibles to **bore**, or dig, into the dying or dead wood of shrubs and trees.*

Outgrowing its skin

As a larva continues to eat, its body grows. Its skin does not grow along with its body, however. The skin gets so tight that the larva must molt. After molting, the larva grows and develops a larger skin. The growing stage between each molt is called an **instar**. Most larvae molt three times, but others molt as many as 29 times.

Most Mexican bean beetle larvae molt four times. Between molts, they eat the leaves and flowers of bean plants.

The pupal stage

Once a larva is fully grown, it starts preparing for the next stage of its life cycle—the pupal stage. Some larvae begin this stage in summer. Larvae that live in areas with cold **climates** become **pupae**, or pupas, in the late fall and remain in this stage during the cold winter.

Stick to it!

Some larvae seek out leaves, stems, trees, or branches on which to hide during the pupal stage. After a larva has found the right spot, it attaches itself to the surface of a plant part.

Making a case

When it is securely attached, the larva molts for the last time. Its new skin gradually hardens, and the larva begins making a hard case for itself. To make the case, it uses material from its body or its surroundings.

Ladybird beetle pupae are almost as big as adult beetles, but they do not look like adults.

Dig in

Some larvae do not attach themselves to leaves or stems. Instead, they make safe, well-hidden **pupal cells**, or cocoons, out of dirt or animal droppings. Some larvae burrow beneath the ground or tunnel under rocks.

Many types of water beetle larvae seal themselves inside small, safe **chambers**, or enclosed areas, made of mud. Inside their pupal cells, burrows, or chambers, these pupae are warm, safe from predators, and have the moisture they need to grow and change.

Most Pennsylvania firefly larvae become pupae in the fall and remain pupae until the spring. This Pennsylvania firefly pupa has found a safe spot among some rocks.

Changing form

Inside their cases, the pupae turn into adult beetles. They lie very still and do not eat during this time. Their bodies are going through metamorphosis. They are changing from one form to another.

Wings, muscles, and more

A pupa's wings and elytra develop during this stage. If the pupa is a flying beetle, it grows the muscles it will need to fly. It also develops the organs it will need to **mate** with other beetles. The beetle's exoskeleton becomes hard and tough during this time as well.

(above) The multicolored Asian ladybird beetle in the middle has finished its metamorphosis. It now has an adult body. The pupae on either side of the adult have not yet completed metamorphosis.

Get me out of here!

Many pupae complete metamorphosis in spring or summer, when the weather provides the right amount of sunlight and rain. The beetle's case splits open, and the beetle is now a fully formed adult.

Cutting their way out

Some adult beetles must use their strong jaws to cut out of their cases and to come up from their burrows and pupal cells. Other beetles have long, sharp mouthparts for cutting their way out of their cocoons. These special mouthparts break off soon after the adult beetles have emerged. Most adult beetles begin looking for food as soon as they cut out of their cases.

Most weevils remain in the pupal stage for ten to sixteen days. A few beetles stay in this stage for up to nine months.

All grown up

A beetle becomes an adult when it has finished growing and is able to make babies. Many become adults a few weeks after they hatch from their eggs. Others take months or years to become adults.

Some species of beetles spend more time living as larvae than as adults. Certain stag beetles can remain in the larval stage for up to five years, but they live only about five months as adults.

The six-spotted green tiger beetle often lives in gardens and forests. It is a fast runner and a good flier. Like all tiger beetles, it is also a fierce hunter.

Male and female

It is often hard to tell male and female beetles apart, but there are some slight differences. Female ground beetles and longhorned beetles are often larger than the males. Male stag beetles, shown below, have larger mandibles than female stag beetles have. Although the mandibles of females are smaller, they are stronger and sharper than those of male stag beetles.

Two male stag beetles sometimes fight each other to mate with a female.

Finding a mate

Most adult beetles are **solitary**, which means they live alone. When it is time to mate, males and females of the same species find one another. Most beetles mate in early spring, but some mate in the fall.

Sounds and scents

Beetles have different ways of finding **mates**, or partners. Some beetles make sounds by rubbing parts of their bodies together or tapping their abdomens against the ground. Females often release chemicals called **pheromones** into the air. Using their antennae, males follow the pheromones. Eventually, the males find the females. Making sounds and giving off scents helps beetles locate one another even when they are far apart.

Long antennae help a beetle locate a mate by detecting the pheromones of other beetles.

Lighting up

Some beetles, including fireflies, glowworms, and click beetles, use light to find mates. These beetles are **bioluminescent**, or able to produce light with their organs. They use their organs to create flashes of light or steady glows. Each type of bioluminescent beetle has a special flash pattern.

These male fireflies are flashing their special flash patterns and waiting for females to flash back.

Fertilizing eggs

Females make eggs in their bodies. A male and female mate so the male can **fertilize** the female's eggs with a liquid called **sperm**. The male's sperm fertilizes the female's eggs so that larvae can grow inside them. Female beetles usually mate only once. They gather enough sperm to fertilize all the eggs in their bodies. The females of most species have a **spermatheca**, or an organ that stores sperm. Each egg is fertilized as it moves past the spermatheca on its way out of the mother's body.

On land and in water

Adult beetles live in many **habitats**. A habitat is the natural place where an animal lives. Beetles live only in places where they are able to find food.

Living on the ground

Many beetles, including ground beetles, live in grass, on forest floors, among stones, under logs, and along the shores of lakes, rivers, or streams. They may even live deep in mud or soil.

Most ground beetles hide under leaves or among sticks during the day and come out at night to eat.

Living on plants and trees

Longhorned beetles, leaf beetles, and bark beetles are some of the species that live on plant leaves and stems and on trees. Bark beetles often live in trees that are weak, dying, or have been recently cut. They live and feed under the bark.

The dogbane beetle feeds on dogbane and milkweed plants.

Living in water

Some beetles live in lakes, rivers, ponds, and streams. In order to breathe, they trap air under their elytra and carry it with them underwater. When these beetles run out of air, they return to the surface for more. Some water beetles have flat, paddle-like hind legs, which help them steer and swim through water. Predacious diving beetles swim by moving their legs one at a time, as though they are running through water.

Whirligig beetles skim the surface of the water or swim together in large groups. They often eat insects that fall onto the water's surface.

Feeding time

Most beetles are **herbivores**, or animals that eat plants. Some beetles are predators. These beetles feed on other insects such as flies and wasps. Other beetles are **scavengers**, which feed on dead or decaying plants and animals.

Tiger beetles use their fast legs to chase prey and capture it with their sharp mandibles. Other predators simply wait for prey to come close enough to catch.

Leaves, wood, and more!

Herbivores eat leaves, flowers, seeds, roots, stems, bark, and wood. Some feed on flower petals, **nectar**, or **pollen**. As these beetles eat, they spread pollen from one flower to another. Spreading pollen helps plants make new seeds.

Chasing after food

Many predators are fast runners and good climbers. These abilities help them chase down and catch their **prey**, or the animals they eat. Beetles that are predators can easily trap slow-moving prey such as snails or slugs. Some types of ground beetles are **omnivores**. Omnivores feed on both plants and animals.

Eating a meal

Beetles that are predators eat their prey in different ways. Many cut their food into tiny pieces, using their mandibles as scissors. Some crush their prey and then suck out their insides. Other beetles use special juices that **dissolve** the prey's soft body parts into a liquid. After the insides are in liquid form, the beetles are able to suck them up.

This beetle has captured a fly. Beetles also feed on ants, crickets, and caterpillars.

Cleaning up

Dung beetles and burying beetles are scavengers. Some dung beetles collect and roll up dung before they eat it. Others feed on droppings wherever they fall. Burying beetles search out dead animals such as mice or rats and bury them. They feed on the **carrion**. By eating animal droppings and carrion, dung and burying beetles help keep natural areas clean.

Beetle defenses

Several animals, including spiders, birds, lizards, small **mammals**, and even other insects, catch and eat beetles. Beetles have many ways of defending themselves against these predators. One way beetles avoid being caught is by staying out of sight. Their small size helps them hide.

When a predator is nearby, most beetles, including the click beetle shown above, lie still or fall to the ground, as though they are dead.

Blending in

Many beetles defend themselves by using **camouflage**. Some beetles have coloring that matches the tree bark on which they climb and feed. Green tortoise beetles, for example, blend in with the green leaves of trees or flowers. Other beetles have patterns and textures on their exoskeletons that resemble lizard or bird droppings. These patterns help them remain hidden on any type of leaf or branch.

Copycats

In order to hide, some beetles **mimic**, or look like, bad-tasting beetles or other insects that bite or sting. Certain types of beetles look like lightning bugs and fireflies, which taste terrible to birds and other predators. A few types of longhorned beetles look like wasps, which can sting predators. Predators are likely to leave these beetles alone.

Looking and flying like a wasp helps the longhorned beetle avoid predators, even though this beetle does not really have a stinger.

Chemical defenses

Some beetles have chemicals in their blood, which they use to **repel**, or keep away, predators. The bombardier beetle stores its chemicals in separate chambers within its body. When these chemicals are combined, they heat up and explode out of the beetle's body in the direction of its enemy. The spray of chemicals often stuns the predator long enough for the beetle to escape unharmed.

Blister beetles have poisonous chemicals in their blood. If the chemicals are released, they can cause blisters on the skin of people and animals.

Dangers to beetles

Even though there are hundreds of thousands of beetles living on Earth, these insects are still in danger. People are their biggest threat. Beetles all over the world are in danger of losing their habitats. Like all animals, beetles die when their natural habitats are polluted. Land, air, and water pollution damage the natural areas where beetles live. People also clear land to make room for cities, farms, and industries. This clearing wipes out the homes of many beetles. Without places to live, feed, and reproduce, beetles are not able to continue their life cycles.

Clearing forests

The world's forests are home to thousands of species of beetles. Many species have not yet been discovered! Several logging and farming companies are cutting down and burning forests at an alarming rate. Once a forest is cleared, it does not grow back. The beetles that live in trees, on forest floors, and under logs lose their habitats. They may even become **extinct**, or gone from Earth.

If forests continue to be cleared, adult stag beetles and their larvae may not have enough rotting wood for food or shelter.

Spraying pesticides

Pesticides are harmful to many insects, including beetles. When people spray plants and crops with pesticides to kill pests such as aphids and flies, they kill beetles, too. Beetles are also threatened by **pesticide drift**, which occurs when wind carries pesticides that are sprayed in one area into areas that were not meant to be sprayed. When pesticides drift, they harm beetles in many areas.

Helping beetles

Many people do not care about beetles because there are so many of them and because they are so small. Some people even fear beetles because they seem creepy. Beetles are, however, important to the environment and to many other animals. Several animals, including birds, lizards, and toads, rely on beetles or beetle larvae for food. Some beetles feed on insects, such as aphids and gypsy moths, which are harmful to the food crops and trees grown by people. The beetles that are scavengers are also important because they eat dead or decaying plants and animals. These beetles help control the amount of waste and carrion on Earth.

Endangered beetles

Some species of beetles, such as the American burying beetle, the northeastern beach tiger beetle, and the coffin cave beetle, are **endangered**, or in danger of dying out. People in several countries have formed groups to protect these and other endangered beetles. These groups work to protect the beetles and their habitats so these insects can continue to live on Earth.

Learn more

One of the easiest ways to help beetles is to learn more about them and how important they are to the environment. To find out more, visit these websites:

- www.ento.csiro.au/education/insects/coleoptera.html
- www.insects.org/entophiles/coleoptera
- www.canadianbiodiversity.mcgill.ca/english/species/insects/coleoptera.htm

Glossary

Note: Boldfaced words that are defined in the book may not appear in the glossary.

abdomen A beetle's rear body section

aphid An insect that eats the sap of plants

camouflage Colors or markings on an animal that hide it in its natural surroundings

carrion Dead or decaying animal flesh

climate The normal weather conditions in an area, including temperature, rainfall, and wind

dissolve To make into liquid

fertilize To add sperm to an egg so a baby can form inside it

mammal A warm-blooded animal that has a backbone

mate To join together to make babies

nectar A sweet liquid in flowers

organ A part of the body, such as a lung, which does an important job

pesticide A chemical that kill insects

pollen A powdery substance found in flowers

sperm A male reproductive cell that joins with a female's egg to produce babies

thorax The part of a beetle's body to which legs and wings are attached

yolk The part of an egg that feeds the growing embryo

Index

1 2 3 4 5 6 7 8 9 0   Printed in the U.S.A.   3 2 1 0 9 8 7 6 5 4